THE MILITARY EXPERIENCE™
Special Operations:
RECONNAISSANCE

THE MILITARY EXPERIENCE.
Special Operations:
RECONNAISSANCE

DON NARDO

MORGAN
REYNOLDS
PUBLISHING

GREENSBORO, NORTH CAROLINA

The Military Experience.
Special Operations: Reconnaissance
Copyright © 2013 by Morgan Reynolds Publishing

For more information write:
Morgan Reynolds Publishing, Inc.
620 South Elm Street, Suite 387
Greensboro, NC 27406 USA

Library of Congress Cataloging-in-Publication Data

Nardo, Don, 1947-
The military experience : special operations : reconnaissance / by
Don
Nardo.
    p. cm.
Includes bibliographical references and index.
ISBN 978-1-59935-366-1 -- ISBN 978-1-59935-367-8 (e-book) 1.
Military
reconnaissance--United States. 2. Special forces (Military
science)--United
States. 3. United States--Armed Forces--Commando troops. I. Title.
U220.N37 2013
355.4'13--dc23

                          2012027952

Printed in the United States of America
First Edition

Book cover and interior designed by:
Ed Morgan, navyblue design studio
Greensboro, NC

Table of Contents

A U.S. Special Forces soldier conducts rehearsal, training, and pre-operation conformation on the MK 12 sniper rifle.

CHAPTER ONE

Secret DATA-gathering in Fallujah

A confirmed insurgent stronghold goes up in smoke after an aerial strike during combat operations while U.S. Marines search for insurgents and weapon caches during Operation al-Fajr in Fallujah, Iraq.

The city of Fallujah, in
Al Anbar Province, Iraq

U.S. Marine Captain Jason Schauble and a handful of fellow Marines sat or crouched silently in their hiding places in an abandoned house. For several hours they watched enemy soldiers moving through the city's streets and kept careful note of what they were doing. At this point, Fallujah was mostly quiet. Schauble and his men were the only ones in town who knew that all hell was about to break loose.

Located in central Iraq, Fallujah has many Muslim mosques. For a long time, therefore, Iraqis thought of it as a holy city, a peaceful place to pray and meditate. That started to change after the United States invaded Iraq in 2003. Iraqi insurgents, fighters loyal to the brutal dictator Saddam Hussein, began flocking to Fallujah. And soon several thousand of them had made it their home base.

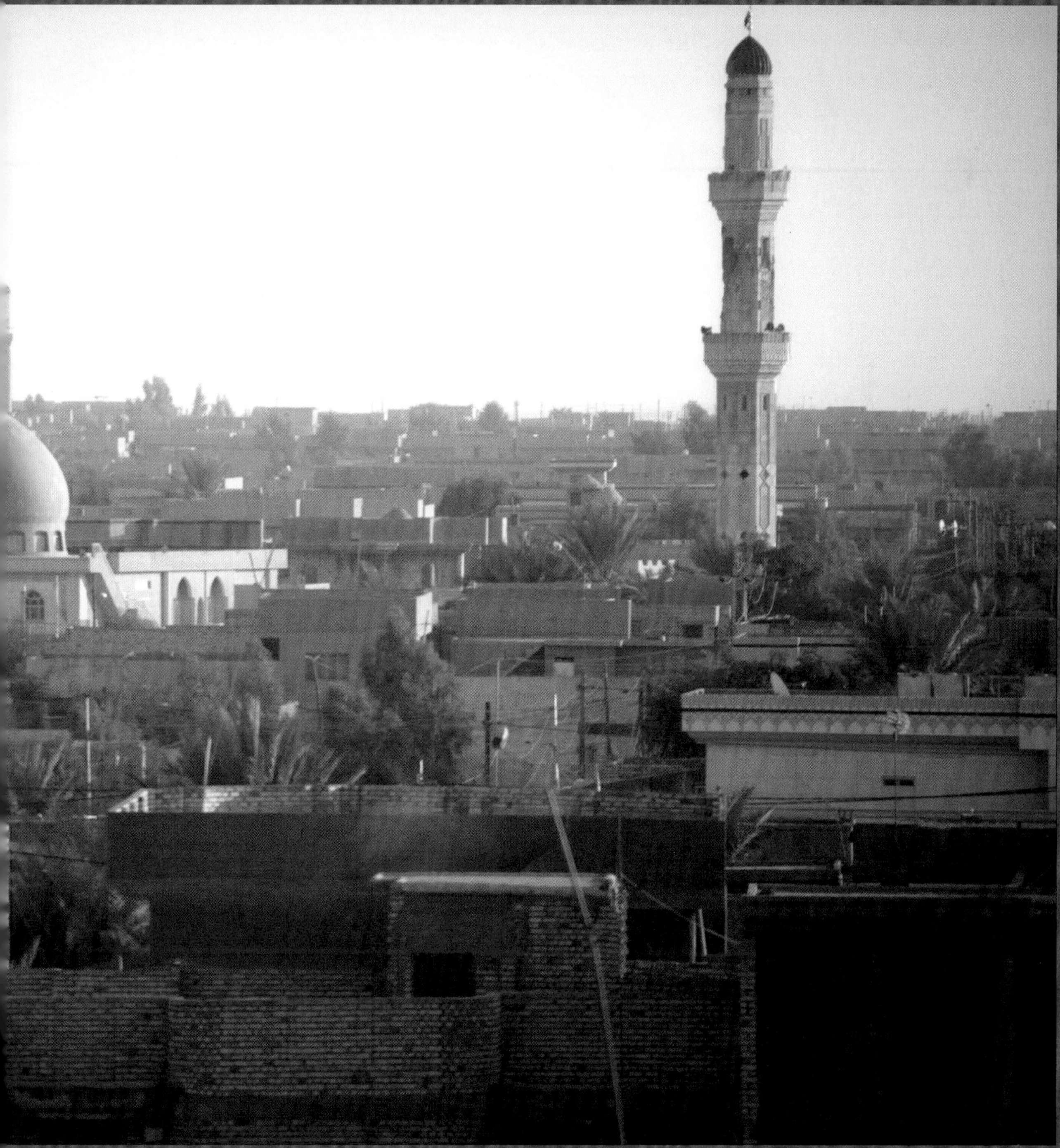

THE ENEMY WITHOUT A CLUE

To eliminate that base, the Americans launched an offensive called Operation Phantom Fury. It called for a few elite fighters—Schauble and his comrades—to sneak into the city. They did so in early November 2004, a few days before the main U.S. attack. Their job was to estimate enemy numbers and scout their positions and activities. That would make it easier later for the main U.S. forces to find and target the insurgents.

Schauble and his men also had orders to kill enemy fighters when possible. That would hopefully keep the insurgents on edge and fearful. To that end, one of the Marines, Sergeant Mark Detrick, set up a tripod in the abandoned house. On this holder he placed his trusty sniper rifle. Then he poked the weapon's barrel through a hole he had earlier drilled in a wall facing the street.

"They don't have a clue what's coming," Detrick told Schauble. The latter nodded and watched Detrick squeeze off a round. The bullet sped outward. Less than a second later it tore through the body of an insurgent, who instantly slumped over dead.

Not long afterward the hidden Marines increased the frequency of their shots. And the insurgents fired back. "We were shooting in all directions," Schauble later recalled. "There were enemies coming out [and] setting up mortars." They also fired "machine guns and small arms. We shot all day, at different targets" as insurgents "in sneakers and track pants scurried from house to house."

These small-scale skirmishes ended on November 8 as U.S. planes began bombing the insurgents. In many cases they knew the exact areas to target, thanks to the secret data-gathering of Schuable's advance group. Also, thousands of American ground troops arrived in the days that followed. In all, some 1,350 Iraqi insurgents were killed. Yet only 95 Americans died, a low figure that U.S. military leaders also partly credited to Schauble and his men. The tiny unit of Marines "provided us with some tremendous capabilities," one American officer remarked. "I just can't say enough about the job they did."

fact BOX

The City of Mosques

The Iraqi city of Fallujah has long been known as the "city of mosques." This is because it once contained more than two hundred mosques. An estimated sixty to sixty-five of these places of worship were destroyed in the American bombing raids in November 2004.

A mosque in Fallujah

Marine Corps Captain Doug Zembiec gives orders to his men over a radio prior to leaving their secured compound for a short patrol in Fallujah, Iraq.

GATHERING INTELLIGENCE

Schauble and his companions completed their difficult mission successfully in part because of their special training. They were members of a small group of Marines called Force Recon (sometimes referred to as FORECON). *Recon* is short for *reconnaissance,* which means "scouting" or "information-gathering." A special recon mission is one in which a small team of soldiers enters enemy territory, usually secretly. Its members observe enemy activities and report what they have learned to their commanders.

Force Recon Marines are not the only U.S. military personnel who do special recon work. Several branches of the military have special ops groups whose members are also trained to do it. (*Special ops* is short for *special operations.*) These select fighters, or commandos, carry out missions that are usually too difficult for ordinary soldiers.

Whichever military branch they belong to, special recon fighters gather "intelligence," or assorted data about an enemy. One aspect of intelligence they look for is how many enemy soldiers exist in a given area. Also, what are those soldiers doing? How well or poorly armed are they? What are their strong and weak points? Perhaps most importantly, what is the most effective way to undermine them?

Such missions are extremely hazardous and risky. But the courageous individuals who carry them out do not shrink from the danger. "We enjoy what we do," Schauble told a reporter after the Fallujah battle. "There's a lot of risks, but we're all volunteers." Later he added humbly, "I do what I do because that's what had to be done at the time."

Green vs. Black Ops

The intelligence-gathering aspects of special recon work are known as "green operations," or "green ops" for short. According to former military police officer Ryan Maxwell, "In green operations, the Marines must use stealth and silence to avoid any contact with the enemy. If discovered or involved in a firefight [battle involving guns], the mission is considered a failure." However, there is a second kind of special recon work called "black ops." Used less often than green ops, it involves "direct action." That is, after the team members have gathered what information they can, their job is not finished. They go on to destroy whatever enemy assets they can. In Fallujah, Jason Schauble's unit was authorized to do black as well as green ops. The shots they took at the insurgents were an example of direct action against an enemy. Other examples of special recon black ops include ambushing an enemy camp, seizing an enemy oil facility, and blowing up enemy tanks or trucks.

A U.S. Marine Corps tank fires its main gun into a building to provide suppressive counter fire against insurgents who fired on other Marines during a fire fight in Fallujah, Iraq.

CHAPTER TWO

Introducing the RECON COMMANDOS

Marines and sailors take part in Training in an Urban Environment Exercise or "TRUEX." The Maritime Special Purpose Force is a composite unit made up of Marines and sailors from the Marine Expeditionary Unit's Battalion Landing Team, 1st Battalion, 5th Marine Regiment, and the command element's Deep and Amphibious Reconnaissance Platoons.

Navy SEALs perform Advanced Cold Weather training to experience the physical stress of the environment and how their equipment will operate, or even sound, in adverse conditions.

The United States military has long recognized the extreme importance of special recon missions. Gathering intelligence about enemy forces has therefore been assigned to several U.S. military units. Their members receive special schooling. In fact, their preparation goes well beyond the basic training given to ordinary soldiers.

That is partly why most special recon missions are carried out by commandos. These elite fighters learn special skills such as survival in extreme situations, evading enemy patrols, and escaping from enemy custody. Special recon work occurs mostly behind enemy lines, where those skills are badly needed. So it seems only natural that such work be done primarily by special ops units.

These exceptional units come from several different branches of the U.S. military. The Navy sometimes needs the kind of information that recon missions provide, and when it does, it most often calls on its SEALs. The term *SEAL* stands for "Sea, Air, Land." In other words, these men are experts in warfare at sea, in the air, and on land.

But though very versatile, more often than not the SEALs take part in amphibious, or water-based, operations. A typical special recon mission for the SEALs begins with their diving beneath the ocean's surface at night. Quiet and unseen, they swim to a beach in enemy territory. There, they may set up an observation station to keep track of enemy movements. Or if necessary they may creep further inland and observe from there.

THE RANGERS, GREEN BERETS, AND DELTA FORCE

The U.S. Army also has commando groups that are trained in reconnaissance. One—the Army Rangers—has traditions of scouting the enemy that go back to Colonial America. Modern Rangers still hold dear the memory of Rogers' Rangers, a famous regiment of specially trained soldiers. Beginning in the 1750s, they conducted raids against Britain's enemies—the French and their Indian allies. Often the Rangers traveled dozens or even hundreds of miles in secret. Entering enemy territory, they gathered intelligence about their opponents before attacking them.

fact BOX

Major Rogers and His Rangers

The Colonial American unit of scouts and wilderness fighters—Rogers' Rangers—was created and commanded by Major Robert Rogers. Some of the group's adventures were portrayed in the stirring 1940 film *Northwest Passage,* with the great Spencer Tracy as Major Rogers.

An illustration depicting Robert Rogers. No actual likenesses exist.

Three U.S. Army Rangers participate in a training exercise.

All modern Army Rangers receive at least some training in recon work. But an elite group of Ranger scouts was introduced in 1984. It is called the Regimental Reconnaissance Detachment (RRD). Its twelve members are organized into three four-man teams. Once behind enemy lines, they report on enemy movements. They also call in U.S. air strikes on nearby enemy targets and place hidden cameras and listening devices near enemy camps or bases.

Another Army commando group—the Green Berets (or Army Special Forces)—is highly adept in recon work. A major task of its members is to sneak into enemy-controlled territory. There, they oppose the local regime in various ways. One of the most important is to gather information about what is happening in local towns and send that information back to U.S. military leaders.

Still another Army special ops group is the mysterious Delta Force. It and its objectives and actions are so secret that few definite facts about it are known. Some military observers contend that members of the group played key roles in the U.S. invasion of Iraq in 2003. Supposedly, they entered the country unseen a few weeks before the main attack. Blending in with the local people, they compiled a list of targets for U.S. planes to bomb and destroyed Iraqi communication lines.

THE COMBAT CONTROLLERS AND FORCE RECON

The Air Force's contribution to the U.S. special recon community is particularly impressive. Members of the group are informally called CCTs, short for Combat Control Technicians (or Teams). These commandos are often the first U.S. personnel to enter enemy territory during a U.S. invasion. They parachute in, unnoticed. Then they set up a secret command post and use advanced radio equipment to let American forces know what the enemy is up to. One Air Force officer says that these commandos undertake "the most dangerous missions behind enemy lines by leading the way for other forces to follow."

No less important than the other American recon experts are the members of the Marines' recon units. The oldest is Force Recon, created in the 1950s. It is made up of highly trained soldiers under the command of the head of the Marine Corps. In contrast, the Marine Special Operations Command (MARSOC) appeared in 2007. Its members are commandos who report to the U.S. Special Operations Command (USSOCOM).

Whether they are members of the SEALs, Rangers, CCTs, Force Recon, or some other group, all U.S reconnaissance experts have two things in common. First, they are among the world's best at what they do. Second, they are fiercely loyal to their country. These qualities make them military assets of the highest order.

Two SEAL team members, one equipped with an AN-PAQ-1 laser target DESIGNATOR (*right*), the other armed with an M-14 rifle, assume a defensive position after assaulting the beach during an amphibious demonstration for the 14th Annual Inter-American Naval Conference at Naval Amphibious Base Little Creek, in Virginia.

Force Recon
vs.
Navy SEALs

Marine Eric O'Neil says he has often met people who do not understand the difference between Force Recon Marines and Navy SEALs. He explains it this way:

> They are similar to the Navy SEALs in that they are heavily trained in airborne and combat diving techniques. . . . The difference between them is that the SEALs' purpose is to kill the enemy, while Force Recon's main purpose is simply to gather intelligence. Force Recon's mission is considered a success if absolutely no shots are fired. Marines in Force Recon are absolutely trained in direct action missions, and are capable of performing in combat situations, but that is not their primary role.

Marines engage a target during a close-quarters battle drill with their .45 caliber pistols. The large-caliber pistol is crucial for the recon Marines' and sailors' direct-action operations as an additional weapon.

CHAPTER THREE

Trained to Survive, Observe, and Report

**Marine Corps's Maritime Special Purpose Force
with a Diver Propulsion Vehicle, or Device**

One important reason that U.S. special recon personnel are so good at their jobs is that they are very well trained. The training they receive in their military careers consists of three general phases. The first, which all members of the U.S. armed forces must undergo, is boot camp. There, they acquire the basics of being in the military. This includes getting into excellent physical shape; learning to follow orders and work as part of a team; becoming proficient with standard military weapons; and learning to fight hand-to-hand without weapons.

Some of the individuals who graduate from boot camp volunteer to join one of the military's special ops groups. It might be the Navy's SEALs or Special Boat sailors; the Air Force's pararescuemen or CCTs; or the Army's Rangers or Green Berets. (One exception is the Marines' Force Recon, which is not classified as special ops.) Only a few of these men make it through commando training, which is extremely hard.

An Explosive Ordnance Disposal team working closely with SEAL team personnel practices Special Insertion and Extraction techniques from an SH-60 Seahawk helicopter.

IN TOP PHYSICAL CONDITION

Among those who do make it through special ops training and become U.S. commandos, a few opt to go on to phase three. It consists of specific training in reconnaissance work. Here again, the instructors look for the best of the best. Simply to be accepted for the training, the recruits must be in top physical condition.

Some idea of what this means can be seen in the case of Marines who desire to join Force Recon. Each man must score a minimum of 275 points in a series of three daunting physical tests. A perfect score is three hundred points, or one hundred points for each test. Someone who can do eighty sit-ups in under two minutes would get one hundred points; doing twenty pull-ups, each from a "dead hang" position, would score one hundred points; and running 3 miles (4.8 km) in under eighteen minutes would earn someone one hundred points. Clearly, only those who are in tremendous physical condition can score the required 275 points.

Physical training continues throughout the recon schooling. Meanwhile, the recruits learn how to excel in the core function of special reconnaissance—gathering information about the enemy. This is very detail-oriented work. That is, those involved must be very observant. They must be able to recognize the various weapons, gear, and vehicles used by enemy forces.

Also, members of reconnaissance units must be able to remember what they have seen and heard and record it using a wide array of techniques. Finally, they must learn to report the data they have gathered to their superiors. This requires close familiarity with radios and antennas, computers and other digital equipment, cameras, telescopes, map-reading, and much more.

fact BOX

Where are They Trained?

The schools that teach commando survival methods are located across the United States. Army survival training occurs near Fort Bragg, North Carolina; Air Force recruits train at Fairchild Air Force Base, near Spokane, Washington; and much of the Navy SEALs' survival training happens in northern Maine.

READY FOR THE UNKNOWN

Another big part of special recon training is learning to survive behind enemy lines. Also, one must be able to deal directly with the enemy if necessary. The military calls this sort of training SERE, short for Survival, Evasion, Resistance, Escape. The recruits learn to survive and do their jobs in a range of different wilderness settings. These include watery environments, such as rivers and swamps; deep forests and jungles; and mountainous terrains.

Whatever the setting, the men must know how to find food and drinking water. They have to know how to erect makeshift huts, called "hides." These will not only shelter them from the elements, but also keep them hidden from the enemy.

In fact, staying unseen by the enemy is one of the most vital skills that special recon experts must attain. Without it, they are much more likely to be captured or killed by those they were sent to spy on. Remaining hidden is best accomplished using camouflage. It consists of patterns and colors that help to make uniforms, gear, and weapons blend in with a given natural setting. The patterns are random and patchy and the colors are most often rustic versions of brown, green, and yellow.

"Camouflage material is colored with dull hues that match the predominant colors of the surrounding environment," one military observer explained. In wooded or jungle terrains, he added:

> Camouflage is typically green and brown, to match the forest foliage and dirt. In the desert, military forces use a range of tan colors. Camouflage for snowy climates is colored with whites and grays. To complete the concealment, soldiers paint their face with colors matching the camouflage material.

Private First Class Joel Graham puts on camouflage paint as his unit prepares to board the ship that will take him to Vieques Island, Puerto Rico, for a joint exercise with the 26th Marine Expeditionary Unit.

Other survival skills recon personnel must acquire include building fires, rock-climbing, first aid, and navigation. "We teach primitive means of making due with what is at arms-reach," a Navy SERE instructor stated. These include, "constructing a fire with flint and steel, what's edible [safe to eat], and how to use a simple piece of metal as a compass." He added, "You never know what's going to happen out there in hostile environments." So special recon trainees "have to be ready for the unknown."

Capture Training

In addition to survival in wilderness settings, special recon recruits learn how to deal with the enemy. They receive instruction in tracking enemy soldiers. In addition, they learn the best ways to avoid capture. There is always the chance, of course, that they might actually be captured during a mission. So the recruits also endure a simulated capture situation in which the "enemy" fighters are played by U.S. special ops instructors.

The captured recruits are "taken to a mock prisoner of war camp," a military observer explained. There, they are "hooded and roped together." They go for several days without food or sleep. In fact, they are treated so harshly that "over the course of [the training] a student typically drops 15 pounds."

U.S. Marines role play during a simulated night raid at Kahuku Training Area Oahu, in Hawaii. The training area serves as a simulated terrorist training camp controlled by opposition forces participating in exercise Rim of the Pacific, the largest international maritime exercise in the waters around the Hawaiian Islands.

CHAPTER FOUR

Common
RECON
Weapons
and Gear

U.S. Marines from 26th Marine Expeditionary Unit secure Roberts International Airport in Liberia during the Second Liberian Civil War in August 2003.

Specialist Nicholas Haney patrols Mosul, Iraq.

Like other members of the U.S. military, those who perform special recon missions have their preferred tools of the trade. Some are weapons. True, in most cases these individuals try to avoid contact and firefights with the enemy. But sometimes such situations are unavoidable. Moreover, occasionally special recon missions call for black ops activity. If so, weapons are a must.

Other tools needed by special recon personnel consist of gear for spying on the enemy. In addition, they carry communications devices. These are required to report the information gathered on the mission to American military authorities.

When trying to decide which items to take on a mission, recon professionals often consider weight a crucial factor. The reason is that it is vital for them to move quickly and nimbly when behind enemy lines. This is not possible if they are loaded down with too much weaponry and gear. So they try to follow the wisdom of an old Marine saying. One version of it goes: "If you can't swim with it, jump with it, or shoot with it, you don't need it!"

One thing these men feel they do need on every mission is at least one trusty firearm for protection. The choice of which gun to use is often a matter of personal taste. Some recon specialists fall back on the most commonly used U.S. military rifle—the M4 carbine assault rifle. It fires from seven hundred to 950 rounds per minute and can do serious damage to opposing forces. Yet it is amazingly light at only 7 pounds (3 kg).

Some other recon personnel, including most members of the Marines' Force Recon, favor the M16A2 assault rifle. It weighs close to 9 pounds (4 kg). The bullets from an M16A2 can travel almost half a mile (.8 km).

Those who execute recon missions are also known to carry sniper rifles. The standard sniper rifle among American special ops groups is the M24. It weighs just over 15 pounds (6.8 kg) and can fire rounds with considerable accuracy as far as 1,500 feet (457 m). Of course, that assumes that the operator has the necessary skills.

OTHER WEAPONS

Members of special recon teams often carry other weapons besides firearms. Force Recon Marines frequently wield large knives known as K-bars, for instance. They are not only handy for defense but also effective for slicing through heavy vegetation in forests or jungles. Indeed, men trying to survive in wilderness situations can generally find numerous practical uses for knives. "I have [a] small knife with a blade of 2.75 inches (7 cm) and an overall length of 7.25 inches (18 cm)," said Marine recon expert Patrick A. Rogers. "It is a strong knife, and very handy for those million and one things that you need a knife for."

It is not unusual for recon professionals to carry explosives as well. This is particularly true when they are ordered to engage in black ops, which can involve blowing up enemy buildings or vehicles. The most common explosive they employ is C4, also called plastique. It has roughly the consistency of modeling clay. So it is easily molded into any desired shape for attaching it to various surfaces. Another benefit is that it can be detonated, or triggered, from a distance.

INSIDE THE RECON TOOLKIT

Peeking inside the recon toolkit, so to speak, one sees much more than weapons used for defense or black ops. There are also numerous devices that allow these men to accomplish their main mission. That task is green ops—gathering intelligence about the enemy and sending it to American leaders. In order to do these things, the recon scouts must remain undetected by that enemy. So they carry with them motion sensors, which they often set up around their temporary secret base. If an enemy soldier or vehicle approaches, those sensors will perceive it and alert the recon team.

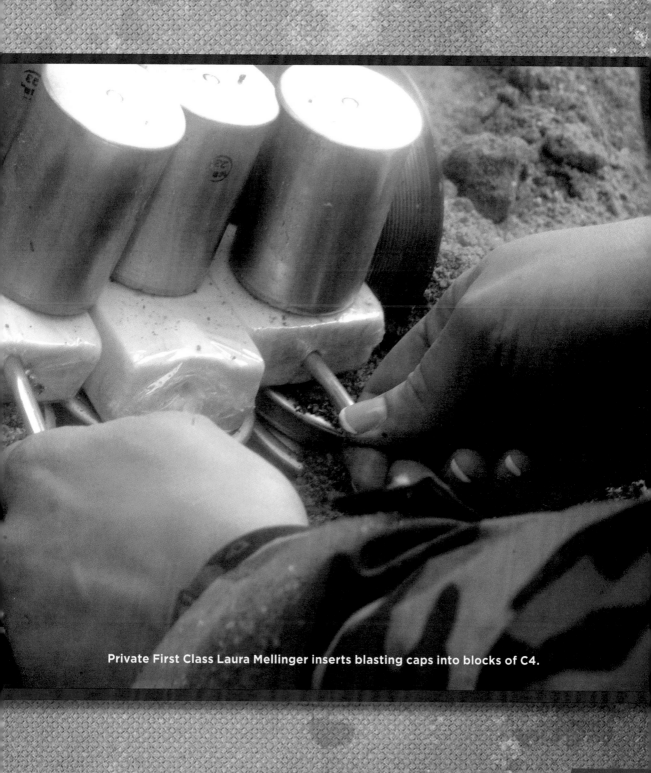

Private First Class Laura Mellinger inserts blasting caps into blocks of C4.

Recon experts also carry portable radios. One use for them is to spy on enemy communications. Another is to send messages to the U.S. officials in charge of the recon operation. In addition, each member of the recon unit has his own headset, allowing him and his comrades to stay in contact when separated by more than a few yards.

Among the many other high-tech devices these men employ are night vision goggles, which allow them to see in the dark. Others include small telescopes for seeing the enemy up close; laptop computers to record information digitally; digital cameras that plug into the laptops; and laser instruments that use beams of light to measure distances precisely.

Such advanced equipment makes reconnaissance work easier and more efficient. Yet it does not ensure that the mission will be successful. The skills and attitude of the men on the team are almost always the deciding factors in that success. As Patrick Rogers points out, "Well-trained and motivated people will do better with mediocre [second-rate] equipment then mediocre people will do with the best gear in the world."

Seen through a night-vision device, paratroopers conduct a raid on a suspected terrorist's home in Fallujah, Iraq.

fact BOX

Protective Clothing

The Americans who carry out special recon missions often wear various kinds of protective clothing. These include vests and helmets made of Kevlar, a substance stronger than steel, and knee and elbow pads to rest on while firing their rifles.

Seabees sprint during a readiness exercise at Naval Construction Battalion Center, in Gulfport, Mississippi. They did a series of activities to become accustomed to wearing a module tactical vest and Kevlar.

Finding One's EXACT LOCATION

U.S. recon personnel carry with them GPS, which stands for Global Positioning System. This device uses several satellites that orbit our planet twice each day. "During this orbiting," one military observer explained, the satellites "transmit precise time, latitude, longitude, and altitude information. Using a GPS receiver," scouts can find "their exact location anywhere on Earth," including their position behind enemy lines.

U.S. Marines at Roberts International Airport in Liberia during the Second Liberian Civil War in 2003

CHAPTER FIVE

Special RECON Warriors in Action

Various units of the U.S. armed forces have carried out thousands of special reconnaissance missions over the years. The exact events of many of these missions remain largely secret. This is because the military, understandably, is cautious. It does not want potential enemies to know the full extent of what American recon personnel are capable of.

Still, the details of some missions *are* known to the public. A brief look at two of them is instructive. First, it shows some typical situations that U.S. special recon units encounter. Second, it confirms that the highly trained members of these units regularly risk their lives to make it more likely that other American soldiers will live.

OBSTACLES IN THE DEPTHS?

One such mission took place in the war-torn nation of Somalia, in East Africa, in December 1992. The year before, that country had fallen into a bloody civil war. And as the months rolled by, large numbers of Somalis became displaced and began to starve.

Worried, a majority of the member states of the United Nations (UN) voted to send peacekeepers to Somalia. Fittingly, they named the plan of action Operation Restore Hope. Part one involved securing the partially destroyed airport in the Somali capital of Mogadishu. A force of U.S. Marines and soldiers from several other nations prepared to land on some nearby beaches. From there, they intended to move directly to the airport.

The problem was that UN and U.S. military planners knew almost nothing about the waters near Mogadishu. How deep were they? Were there harmful obstacles lurking in the depths? The planners did not want to risk the lives of the Marines and other troops by sending them into a potentially dangerous situation. So they sent a team of Navy SEALs on a special recon mission.

The SEALs donned their scuba gear and slipped beneath the waves off the Somali shore. First, they carefully measured the water depth at various points along the coast. This would help the UN peacekeepers to make a safer landing. The SEALs also explored Mogadishu Harbor to see if it was safe for UN and U.S. ships to dock there. What they found was deeply disturbing. The harbor's water was badly poisoned by raw sewage and other wastes. The water was so contaminated, in fact, that some of the SEALs became very ill.

Despite this setback, the next day another team of SEALs joined with a team of Force Recon Marines. These intrepid scouts swam ahead of the main landing forces to make sure the way was clear. Thanks in large part to their courageous efforts, the landings were successful.

An aerial view of the Port of Mogadishu, in Somalia

An M1A1 Abrams main battle tank lays a smoke screen during maneuvers during Operation Desert Storm.

A PROUD LEGACY

Another example of U.S. recon scouts leading the way for a main body of military forces occurred in Kuwait and Iraq in 1990-1991. The conflict became known as the Persian Gulf War. Iraq's dictator, Saddam Hussein, invaded and captured the tiny neighboring country of Kuwait. And along with Britain and other allies, the United States decided to free Kuwait.

In this case, many of the special recon teams were made up of CCTs, the Air Force's Combat Controllers. Their first task was to survey possible landing sites for allied planes and helicopters. At great risk to themselves, the CCTs parachuted into areas behind enemy lines and quietly blended with their surroundings. In all, they looked at more than two hundred potential landing sites. They also coordinated some 1,650 plane landings in a mere ten days.

In addition, the CCTs helped Army and Marine scouts to get a convoy of Americans and their allies through a region filled with mines and unexploded bombs. "In one instance," military observer James Thede recalled, "a team of controllers was placed" at the front "of a 165-vehicle" Army convoy. "The CCT Humvee led the scouts" to a pre-chosen point, "where they would wait for another scout vehicle to race back to the [army's] main body. Once the main body arrived at the point, the scouts," led by the CCTs, "would carefully proceed to the next waypoint."

In each cycle, the scouts located mines and other explosives and showed the soldiers in the army's main body how to avoid them. That allowed U.S. and allied forces to make their way intact across hostile territory. "The CCT/scout relationship was invaluable to the drive to liberate Kuwait," Thede pointed out. "Not enough can be said about the confidence and leadership abilities of the young CCTs" who "led entire U.S. [Army and Marine] divisions across the desert."

It was one of the finest of many fine moments for U.S. special recon units. As in so many other instances through the years, Thede wrote, "small teams of silent professionals doing classified missions" produced an impressive and "proud legacy."

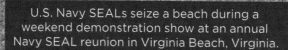

U.S. Navy SEALs seize a beach during a weekend demonstration show at an annual Navy SEAL reunion in Virginia Beach, Virginia.

fact BOX

CCTs in the Gulf War

During the Persian Gulf War, Air Force Combat Control Technicians did recon work in southern Iraq at night. They radioed the data they gathered to special communications planes—called AWACS—that flew high overhead.

Luxembourgian-registered NATO E-3 AWACS flying with three American Air Force F-16 Fighting Falcon fighter aircraft in a NATO exercise

What OTHERS can only IMAGINE

One of the great strengths of the members of U.S. special recon units is their sense of devotion to duty and country. Among these units, those of the Marines' Force Recon have expressed that devotion in the so-called "Recon Creed." It says in part:

> Realizing it is my choice and my choice alone to be a Reconnaissance Marine, I accept all challenges involved with this profession. Forever shall I strive to maintain the tremendous reputation of those who went before me. . . . Never shall I forget the principles I accepted to become a Recon Marine. Honor, Perseverance, Spirit and Heart. A Recon Marine can speak without saying a word and achieve what others can only imagine.

Two SEALs aiming their weapons

Source Notes

Chapter 1: Secret Data-gathering in Fallujah

p. 12, "They don't have a clue . . ." Patrick J. McDonnell, "Marines of Force Recon Set the Stage in Fallouja," *Los Angeles Times*, December 6, 2004, http://articles.latimes.com/2004/dec/06/world/fg-recon6.

p. 12, "We were shooting . . ." Ibid.

p. 12, "provided us with some . . ." Ibid.

p. 15, "We enjoy what we do . . ." Ibid.

p. 15, "I do what I do . . ." April's Insider Report, "Risking His life for His Marines," September 7, 2006, http://insider-report.blogspot.com/2006/09/risking-his-life-for-his-marines.html.

p. 16, "In green operations . . ." Ryan Maxwell, "What is a Recon Mission for the Marines?," http://www.ehow.com/about_5052331_recon-mission-marines.html.

Chapter 2: Introducing the Recon Commandos

p. 24, "the most dangerous missions . . ." The Official Web site of the U.S. Air Force, "Combat Controllers," http://www.af.mil/information/factsheets/factsheet.asp?id=174.

p. 27, "They are similar to . . ." Eric O'Neil, "Where Does Marine Force Recon Fit In the World of Special Operations?," *Forbes*, March 1, 2012, http://www.forbes.com/sites/quora/2012/03/01/where-does-marine-force-recon-fit-in-the-world-of-special-operations/.

Chapter 3: Trained to Survive, Observe, and Report

p. 33, "Camouflage material is colored . . ." Tom Harris, "How Military Camouflage Works," http://science.howstuffworks.com/military-camouflage1.htm.

p. 34, "We teach primitive means . . ." Navy News Service, "Navy SERE Training: Learning to Return with Honor," http://usmilitary.about.com/od/navytrng/a/sere.htm.

P. 34,   "taken to a mock . . ." U.S. Army Special Forces, "Survival Training," http://www.training.sfahq.com/survival_training. htm.

Chapter 4: Common Recon Weapons and Gear

p. 39,   "If you can't swim . . ." Patrick A. Rogers, "Strong Men Armed: The Marine Corps 1st Force Reconnaissance Company," http:// www.forcerecon.com/strongmenarmed3.htm.

p. 40,   "I have [a] small knife . . ." Ibid.

p. 42,   "Well-trained and motivated people . . ." Rogers, "Strong Men Armed."

p. 45,   "During this orbiting . . ." Fred J. Pushies, *Special Ops: America's Elite Forces in 21st Century Combat* (St. Paul: MBI, 2003), 56.

Chapter 5: Special Recon Warriors in Action

p. 51,   "In one instance . . ." James J. Thede, "Combat Control History," Specialtactics.com, June 1, 2007, http://www.specialtactics. com/ccthistory.shtml.

p. 52,   "The CCT/scout relationship . . ." Ibid.

p. 52,   "Small teams of silent professionals . . ." Ibid.

p. 55,   "Realizing it is my choice . . ." Official U.S. Marine Corps Web site, "Recon Creed," http://www.marines.mil/ unit/2ndmardiv/2ndrecon/Pages/mission.aspx.

Glossary

amphibious: Sea-going; or having to do with water.

automatic weapon: A machine gun or other weapon that fires a burst of bullets when the shooter squeezes the trigger.

beret: A small cloth cap worn by members of the Army Special Forces.

C4 (or plastique): A highly destructive explosive substance.

camouflage: Patterns and colors designed to make military uniforms, gear, and weapons blend in with a given natural setting.

CCT: Short for Combat Control Technician (or Team), a type of U.S. Air Force commando.

civilian: A person who is not in the armed forces.

commando: An elite, specially trained soldier who is assigned to difficult, dangerous missions.

environment: A specific natural setting.

convoy: A group of ships or vehicles traveling together.

dead-hang position: Hanging from a horizontal bar with one's arms completely outstretched.

firefight: A battle involving firearms.

flint: A kind of rock that gives off a spark when rubbed against another rock.

GPS (Global Positioning System): A network of orbiting satellites that allow people to quickly compute their exact position on Earth's surface.

hide: A makeshift shelter constructed in the woods or another wilderness area.

intelligence: Information about one's enemies.

K-bar: A large knife carried by many Marines.

Kevlar: A rugged cloth-like material that is five times stronger than steel.

magazine (or clip): A small container inside a gun that holds the bullets.

navigation: Methods of finding one's location and plotting the way from one place to another.

reconnaissance (or recon for short): Scouting, investigating, and/or information-gathering.

recruit: A soldier, sailor, or other fighter who is in training.

regime: A government or ruling group.

round: A bullet or other projectile fired from a gun.

special ops: Short for Special Operations Forces, consisting of the U.S. military's elite units of soldiers.

versatile: Multi-talented.

Bibliography

Cooke, Tim. *U.S. Army Special Forces.* New York: Powerkids Press, 2012.

Clark, Josh. "How the Army Rangers Work." http://science.howstuffworks.com/army-ranger4.htm.

De Lisle, Mark. *Special Ops Fitness Training: High-Intensity Workouts of Navy SEALS, Delta Force, Marine Force Recon, and Army Rangers.* Berkely, CA: Ulysses Press, 2008.

Labrecque, Ellen. *Special Forces.* Mankrato, MN: Heinemann-Raintree, 2012.

Loria, Laura. *Marine Force Recon.* New York: Gareth Stevens, 2012.

McGrath, John J. *Scouts Out! The Development of Reconnaissance Units in Modern Armies.* Charleston, SC: CreateSpace, 2012.

Montana, Jack. *Navy SEALs.* Broomall, PA: Mason Crest, 2011.

Nagle, Jeanne. *Delta Force.* New York: Gareth Stevens, 2012.

Poolos, Jamie. *Army Rangers: Surveillance and Reconnaissance for the U.S. Army.* New York: Rosen, 2003.

Pushies, Fred J. *Marine Force Recon.* St. Paul: MBI, 2003.

Rogers, Patrick A. "Strong Men Armed: The Marine Corps 1st Force Reconnaissance Company." http://www.forcerecon.com/strongmenarmed3.htm.

Sandler, Michael. *Army Rangers in Action.* New York: Bearport, 2008.

———. *Marine Force Recon in Action.* New York: Bearport, 2008.

Smith, Stew. "The Recon Marines." http://www.military.com/NewContent/0,13190,Smith_112003,00.html.

Voeller, Edward. *Recon Marines.* Mankrato, MN: Capstone, 2000.

Web sites

Army Enhanced Night Vision Goggles
http://www.army.mil/article/18980/army-fielding-enhanced-night-vision-goggles/

Army Special Forces Center
http://www.military.com/army-special-forces/training.html

Become a Combat Controller
http://usafcca.org/cca/careers/

Official Web site of the Navy SEALs and SWCC
http://www.sealswcc.com/

Official Web site of SEAL Team Six
http://sealteamsix.net/

Special Reconnaissance: Going Behind Enemy Lines Without Detection.
http://www.goarmy.com/special-forces/primary-missions/special-reconnaissance.html

U.S. Marine Corps Forces Special Operations Command
http://www.marines.mil/unit/marsoc/Pages/default.aspx

Weapons of the Special Forces
http://www.popularmechanics.com/technology/military/1281576

Index

Photo Credits

All images used in this book that are not in the public domain are credited in the listing that follows:

Cover: Courtesy of U.S. Army
6-7: Courtesy of U.S. Navy
8-9: Courtesy of U.S. Marine Corps
10-11: Courtesy of U.S. Marine Corps
13: Courtesy of U.S. Marine Corps
14: Courtesy of U.S. Marine Corps
16-17: Courtesy of U.S. Department of Defense
18-19: Courtesy of U.S. Marine Corps
20-21: Courtesy of U.S. Navy
23: Courtesy of U.S. Department of Defense
25: Courtesy of U.S. Navy
26: Courtesy of U.S. Marine Corps
28-29: Courtesy of U.S. Marine Corps
30: Courtesy of U.S. Navy
33: Courtesy of U.S. Department of Defense
35: Courtesy of U.S. Navy
36-37: Courtesy of U.S. Marine Corps
38: Courtesy of U.S. Air Force
41: Courtesy of U.S. Navy
43: Courtesy of U.S. Department of Defense
44: Courtesy of U.S. Navy
46-47: Courtesy of U.S. Marine Corps
49: Courtesy of Department of Defense
50: Courtesy of Department of Defense
52: Courtesy of U.S. Navy
54: Courtesy of U.S. Military
56-57: Courtesy of U.S. Military